Children's Authors

Marjorie Weinman Sharmat

Jill C. Wheeler
ABDO Publishing Company

Cover Photo: Random House
Interior Photos: Corbis pp. 7, 11, 12, 13; Index Stock p. 9; Random House pp. 5, 23

Editors: Heidi M. Dahmes, Stephanie Hedlund, Megan Murphy
Art Direction: Neil Klinepier

Library of Congress Cataloging-in-Publication Data

Wheeler, Jill C., 1964-
   Marjorie Weinman Sharmat / Jill C. Wheeler.
      p. cm. -- (Children's authors)
   Includes index.
   Summary: Presents the life and work of this author of more than one hundred books for
children and young adults, who is best known for her series of "Nate the Great" books.
   ISBN 1-59197-608-1
   1. Sharmat, Marjorie Weinman--Juvenile literature. 2. Authors, American--20th century--
Biography--Juvenile literature. 3. Children's stories--Authorship--Juvenile literature. [1.
Sharmat, Marjorie Weinman. 2. Authors, American. 3. Women--Biography.] I. Title. II. Series.

PS3569.H34315Z96 2004
813'.54--dc22
[B]
                                                                        2003063876

Contents

Marjorie Weinman Sharmat

Marjorie Weinman Sharmat has written more than 100 popular books for children and young adults. Many of these books have received honors and awards. Some were made into movies and plays. One play was even performed at the White House.

Sharmat is best known for her Nate the Great series. It contains more than 20 books about a young, pancake-eating detective. However, Sharmat has written many other books and articles.

In fact, Sharmat writes for all age-groups. Middle schoolers enjoy several series, including The Kids on the Bus and Maggie Marmelstein books. Young adults read her novels, as well as her Sorority Sisters series.

Sharmat's books have been published in 13 countries. The Nate the Great series has been translated into 11 different languages. Readers and **critics** alike appreciate Sharmat's books for their **readability** and humor.

Opposite page: *Marjorie Weinman Sharmat*

Writer in Training

Marjorie Weinman was born on November 12, 1928, in Portland, Maine. Her father, Nathan, was a businessman. His company made and sold dry goods and menswear. Her mother, Anna, stayed home with Marjorie and her sister, Rosalind.

Marjorie was a shy child. She was often found playing the piano or drawing pictures alone. Marjorie also enjoyed reading, especially fiction books.

During her time alone, Marjorie dreamed about what she would be when she grew up. Part of her wanted to be a writer or a detective. But, she also thought about being a lion tamer.

When she was eight years old, Marjorie focused her efforts on writing. She and a friend started a newspaper called the *Snooper's Gazette*. They did not sell many copies, however. In fact, the newspaper had just four readers! They were the parents of Marjorie and her friend.

As she grew older, Marjorie continued writing stories, songs, and poems. In high school, she wrote for the school newspaper and magazine. She also sent many stories to publishers. Even when her work was turned down, Marjorie's parents encouraged her to keep writing.

Marjorie grew up in Portland, Maine. Her first poem was about a neighborhood dog. Many years later, the poem appeared in her book **The Lancelot Closes at Five.**

Slogans and Stories

Marjorie graduated from high school in 1946. That fall, she took classes at Lasell Junior College in Auburndale, Massachusetts. She transferred to Westbrook Junior College in Portland, Maine, the following year.

At Westbrook, Marjorie studied **merchandising**. She thought it would be a practical career. Marjorie's first job after college was at a department store. For a time, she also wrote the content for greeting cards.

Marjorie remembers that her first published work was a four-word **slogan** for the W.T. Grant Company. She enjoyed seeing the slogan she had written.

In 1951, Marjorie left the **retail** business and moved to New Haven, Connecticut. There, she took a job at Yale University Library. Later, she worked for Yale Law Library. Both jobs were in the **circulation** department.

Marjorie continued writing while working at Yale. Eventually, she had a short story for adults accepted for publication. She later published a story about Yale. It ended up as part of the Yale **Memorabilia** collection. This is a permanent collection at the university.

At Yale Law Library, Sharmat worked at the circulation desk. This station keeps track of the books being checked out. Today, Yale's Lillian Goldman Law Library contains more than 800,000 items.

Mom and Author

Marjorie worked for Yale University until 1955. Two years later, she married Mitchell Sharmat. She and Mitchell had two sons, Craig and Andrew. Marjorie often read to her children. Then, she began writing stories of her own.

In 1967, Marjorie published her first children's book. It was called *Rex*. The story is about a runaway boy who pretends to be a neighbor's dog. Marjorie's sons inspired her to write *Rex*. In real life, Craig often visited their neighbors, and Andrew pretended to be a dog.

Marjorie's second book also took a page from the lives of her sons. One night, she overheard them talking before bedtime. Craig wished his brother "pleasant **nightmares**." The result was a funny book called *Goodnight Andrew, Goodnight Craig*. It was published in 1969.

Rex and *Goodnight Andrew, Goodnight Craig* sold many copies. Marjorie was well on her way to a career as a children's author.

Like this mother, Marjorie read to her children. However, she decided to start writing stories for them as well.

Nate the Great

After the success of her first books, Sharmat began writing about a new character. She had never quite lost her childhood interest in becoming a detective. So, she developed *Nate the Great*. The book is about a young boy named Nate who solves mysteries.

In the 1970s, there were few easy-reader books available. Sharmat wrote *Nate the Great* to be both entertaining and easy to read. *Nate the Great* was released in 1972. It soon became a favorite among children, parents, and librarians.

The Museum of Science and Industry explores the learning process. Nate the Great is part of an exhibit there.

Since then, Sharmat has written 24 Nate the Great mysteries. Most were inspired by real events in her family's life. She has also named many of her characters after family members.

In fact, Sharmat named Nate after her father, Nathan. After the book was published, Nathan was called Nate the Great by friends. Sadly, he died before Sharmat wrote her second Nate the Great book. Sharmat says she continues the series because it is based on a wonderful man.

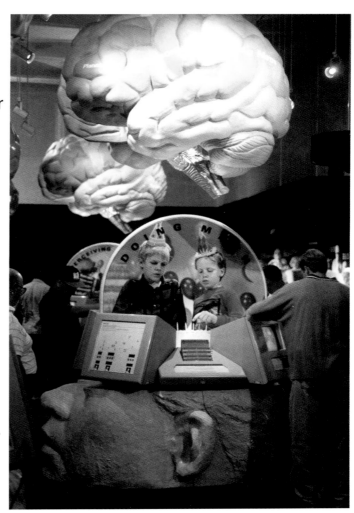

The Museum of Science and Industry is in Chicago, Illinois. Children can visit Nate at the museum's exhibit on the brain.

Writing for All Ages

Sharmat's Nate the Great books were aimed at beginning readers. Yet, she has written several series for middle readers. Maggie Marmelstein was an early series for this reading level. Later series include Rich Mitch and The Kids on the Bus.

In 1975, the Sharmats moved from New York City to Tucson, Arizona. This led Sharmat to write a book about the fear of moving. It was called *Gila Monsters Meet You at the Airport.*

Gila Monsters Meet You at the Airport won two awards. And, it was later made into a television **pilot**. The pilot was for the *Reading Rainbow* program on the Public Broadcasting Service (PBS).

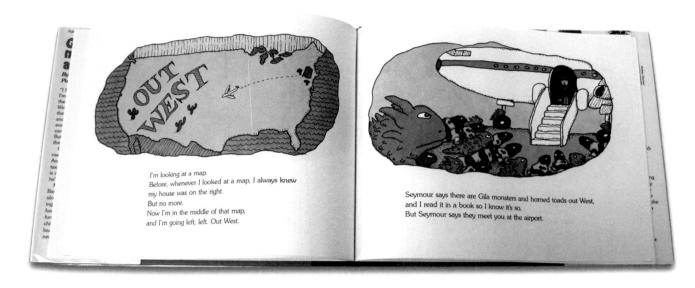

I'm looking at a map.
Before, whenever I looked at a map, I always knew
my house was on the right.
But no more.
Now I'm in the middle of that map,
and I'm going left, left. Out West.

Seymour says there are Gila monsters and horned toads out West,
and I read it in a book so I know it's so.
But Seymour says they meet you at the airport.

Sharmat often writes stories that explore what her characters are feeling.

In 1982, Sharmat began writing books for young adults.
She published *How to Meet a Gorgeous Girl* in 1984. In 1986
and 1987, Sharmat wrote an eight-book series about **campus**
romances called Sorority Sisters.

A Family Affair

Sharmat's family often helps her when she writes. Her sister, Rosalind, has helped her with several Nate the Great books. Andrew was the primary writer for The Kids on the Bus series. And Craig helped her with several Nate books, including *Nate the Great and the Crunchy Christmas*.

Even Mitchell has contributed to her stories. Sharmat says her husband is always the first to edit her books. He often provides just the right line or story idea. Because Mitchell has had so many good ideas, Sharmat told him he should write his own books.

In 1979, Mitchell decided to do just that. Since then, he has published many books. His most famous is *Gregory, the Terrible Eater*.

In 1989, Marjorie and Mitchell began working together on a new detective series. It featured a girl detective named Olivia Sharp. The series is called Olivia Sharp, Agent for Secrets.

Mitchell also co-wrote several Nate the Great books. One is *Nate the Great, San Francisco Detective*. In this book, Nate travels to San Francisco, California, to meet his cousin Olivia Sharp. Together, they solve a mystery.

Sharmat has written more than a hundred books for children of all ages.

Basket of Ideas

Sharmat's books continue to entertain readers. Some people think it would be hard for Sharmat to keep writing. Yet, she says she never runs out of book ideas.

Sharmat compares her brain to a basket that catches a little of everything she sees and feels. The basket ends up containing many different ideas. Then, it is her job to take that material and create a story.

Sharmat works hard to find combinations that make interesting and believable stories. She especially likes them to be funny. Sharmat says life is serious, and it needs some laughter in it to balance things out.

Because of this, Sharmat's writing features her **trademark** sense of humor and believable characters. In addition to books, Sharmat has contributed many articles to magazines, newspapers, and textbooks. She is now in her 70s and still enjoys writing.

Readers enjoy Nate the Great's cases, which are created from events that have happened in Sharmat's life.

No Slowing Down

Reviewers have praised Sharmat's books because they inspire children to follow their curiosity and imagination. Over the years, Sharmat has been honored with many awards.

Sharmat received the Book of the Year award from the Library of Congress three times. *Nate the Great Saves the King of Sweden* has been placed on the New York Public Library's 100 Titles for Reading and Sharing.

In 2002, a special thirtieth-**anniversary** edition of *Nate the Great* was released. Sharmat's most recent Nate the Great title appeared in October 2003. In *Nate the Great on the Owl Express*, Nate is traveling with his cousin Olivia's owl. When the owl disappears, Nate and his dog, Sludge, must find it.

Sharmat never thought *Nate the Great* would become a series. She says she has no idea what will happen next to the pancake-eating detective. Instead she says Nate writes himself, book by book. Young readers can't wait for the next case.

There are 24 books in the Nate the Great series. And though **Nate the Great** *was published in 1972, it is still a favorite among young readers.*

Glossary

anniversary - a celebration of an important event.

campus - the grounds and buildings of a school, university, or college.

circulation - passage from person to person or place to place.

critic - a professional who gives his or her opinion on art or performances.

memorabilia - items that are collected for their connection to a place, thought, or career.

merchandising - sales promotion that includes market research, product development, and advertising.

nightmare - a frightening dream.

pilot - a television show created as a sample of a proposed series.

readability - the degree to which something, such as a book or text, is able to be read and understood.

retail - of or relating to the selling of goods.

slogan - a word or phrase used to express a position, a stand, or a goal.

trademark - a characteristic used to connect an idea or item with a certain person.

Web Sites

To learn more about Marjorie Weinman Sharmat, visit ABDO Publishing Company on the World Wide Web at **www.abdopub.com**. Web sites about Sharmat are featured on our Book Links page. These links are routinely monitored and updated to provide the most current information available.

Index